At Sylvan, we believe reading is one of life's most important and enriching abilities, and we're glad you've chosen our resources to help your child build these critically important skills. We know that the time you spend with your child reinforcing the lessons learned in school will contribute to his love of reading. This love of reading will translate into academic achievement. A successful reader is ready for the world around him, ready to do research, ready to experience the world of literature, and prepared to make the connections necessary to achieve in school and in life.

We use a research-based, step-by-step process in teaching reading at Sylvan that includes thought-provoking reading selections and activities. As students increase their success as readers they become more confident. With increasing confidence, students build even more success. Our Sylvan workbooks are designed to help you to help your child build the skills and confidence that will contribute to your child's success in school.

Included with your purchase of this workbook is a coupon for a discount at a participating Sylvan center. We hope you will use this coupon to further your child's academic journey. Let us partner with you to support the development of a confident, well prepared, independent learner.

The Sylvan Team

1st Grade
Spelling Games & Activities

Published in the United States by Random House, Inc., New York, and in Canada by Random House of Canada Limited, Toronto.

www.tutoring.sylvanlearning.com

Created by Smarterville Productions LLC
Producer: TJ Trochlil McGreevy
Producer & Editorial Direction: The Linguistic Edge
Writer: Sandy Damashek
Cover and Interior Illustrations: Duendes del Sur
Layout and Art Direction: SunDried Penguin
Art Manager: Adina Ficano

First Edition

ISBN: 978-0-375-43025-1

Library of Congress Cataloging-in-Publication Data available upon request.

This book is available at special discounts for bulk purchases for sales promotions or premiums.
For more information, write to Special Markets/Premium Sales, 1745 Broadway, MD 6-2,
New York, New York 10019 or e-mail specialmarkets@randomhouse.com.

PRINTED IN CHINA

10 9 8 7 6 5 4 3 2

Contents

Spell Short A

Slide Words

Let's make words that have a short **a** sound. DRAW a line between each picture and the ending that matches. Then WRITE the first letter of each word.

r am
1

at
2

ap
3

an
4

Fast Words

Can you SAY this sentence three times fast? Try it!

Pat's fat cat sat.

Now WRITE your own sentence. Use these words or other short **a** words. You can use words more than once. Then SAY the sentence three times fast!

ran   and   the   ram   man

_____

_____

_____

Letter Ladder

Let's make more words with the short **a** sound. IDENTIFY the pictures on the ladder. Then WRITE the words next to the pictures.

HINT: You can change just one letter to make each new word.

r a m
1

a
2

a
3

a
4

Around We Go!

CIRCLE the things that have a short **a** sound.

WRITE the words with short **a** on the lines.

_____   _____   _____

_____   _____   _____

_____   _____   _____

Make It Rhyme

CIRCLE the picture that makes a rhyme. WRITE the rhyming word in the space.

The ram eats a _____ .
1

The fan cools the _____ .
2

The hat is on the _____ .
3

Space Walk Words

Make three-letter words with short **a**. START on a blue planet. GO to the green planet. Then GO to another blue planet.

Example:

b a t

WRITE the words here.

_____   _____   _____

_____   _____   _____

Slide Words

Let's make words that have a short **e** sound. DRAW a line between each picture and the ending that matches. Then WRITE the first letter of each word.

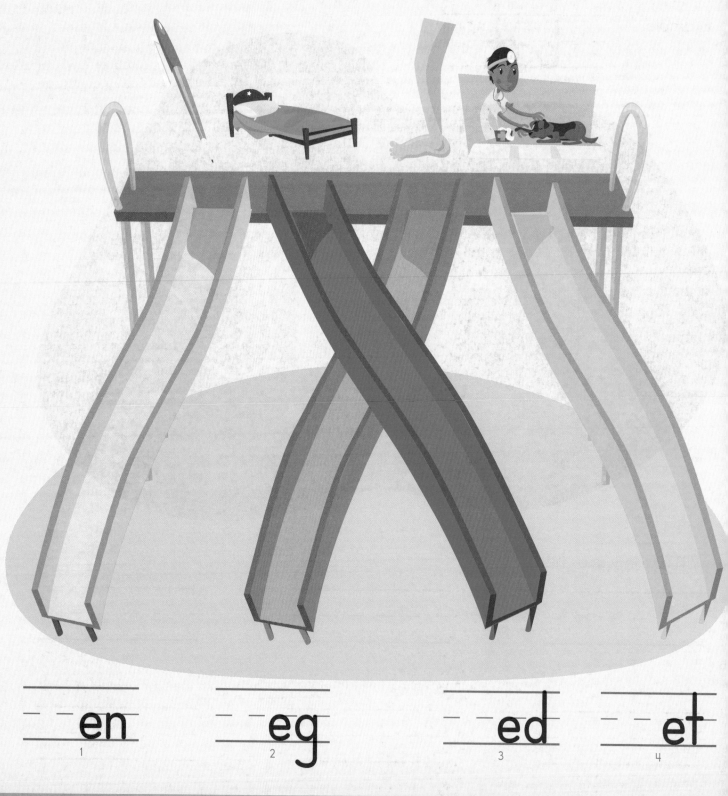

en
1

eg
2

ed
3

et
4

Letter Liftoff

FILL IN the first letter of each short **e** word.

Around We Go!

CIRCLE the things that have a short **e** sound.

WRITE the words with short **e** on the lines.

_____   _____   _____

_____   _____   _____

_____

Fast Words

Can you SAY this sentence three times fast? Try it!

Ten men fed ten hens.

Now WRITE your own sentence. Use these words or other short **e** words. Then SAY the sentence three times fast!

| red | have | beds | legs | red |

_____

- -

_____

- -

_____

Spell Short E

Make It Rhyme

CIRCLE the picture that makes a rhyme. WRITE the rhyming word in the space.

The wet pet saw the _____ . ¹

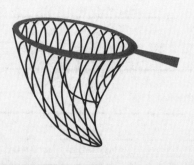

The hen has a _____ . ²

The bed was _____ . ³

12

Space Walk Words

Make three-letter words with short **e**. START on a blue planet. GO to the green planet. Then GO to another blue planet.

WRITE the words here.

_____   _____   _____

- - - - - - - - - - -   - - - - - - - - - - -   - - - - - - - - - - -

_____   _____   _____

- - - - - - - - - - -   - - - - - - - - - - -   - - - - - - - - - - -

_____   _____   _____

How Many at the Market?

How many things can we buy at the market? WRITE a number word under each food.

| one | two | three | four | five | six | seven | eight |

one
1

_____
2

_____
3

_____
4

_____
5

_____
6

_____
7

_____
8

Perfect Landing

DRAW a line between each word and its missing vowel. WRITE the vowel in the space.

Soccer Star

DRAW a line between each picture and the matching vowel. WRITE the words in the nets.

Alphabet Soup

Use the letters in the soup to WRITE the number words. CROSS OUT each letter in the soup after you use it.

Word Hunt

CIRCLE the **number** words in the grid. WRITE each word after you circle it. Words go across and down.

one	two	three	four	five	six	seven	eight	nine	ten

```
n  f  s  e  v  e  n  p  i  h  n  e
f  o  n  e  h  i  f  x  m  q  i  k
h  u  f  c  d  g  i  b  t  s  n  b
y  r  t  e  n  h  v  d  w  i  e  h
t  h  r  e  e  t  e  h  o  x  j  t
```

Slide Words

Let's make words that have a short i sound. DRAW a line between each picture and the ending that matches. Then WRITE the first letter of each word.

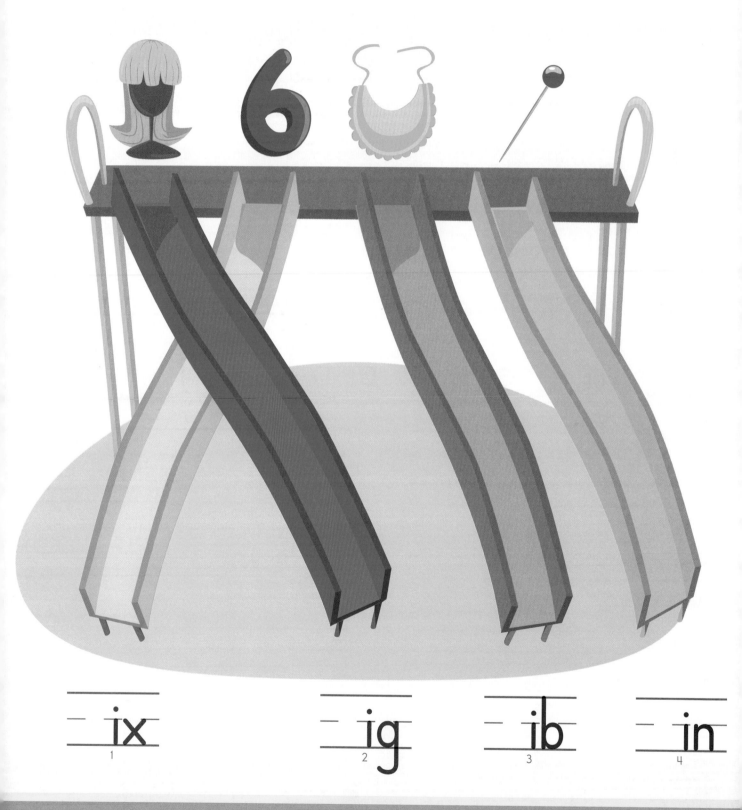

ix
1

ig
2

ib
3

in
4

Around We Go!

CIRCLE the things that have a short **i** sound.

WRITE the words with short **i** on the lines.

_____   _____   _____

Spell Short I

Fast Words

Can you SAY this sentence three times fast? Try it!

Six big pigs sit.

Now WRITE your own sentence. Use these words or other short **i** words. Then SAY the sentence three times fast!

pigs   kids   big   dig

_____

_ _ _ _ _ _ _ _ _ _ _ _ _ _ _ _ _ _ _ _

_____

_ _ _ _ _ _ _ _ _ _ _ _ _ _ _ _ _ _ _ _

_____

Letter Ladder

Let's make more words with the short i sound. IDENTIFY the pictures on the ladder. Then WRITE the words next to the pictures.

HINT: You can change just one letter to make each new word.

1 ¡

2 ¡

3 ¡

4 ¡

Make It Rhyme

CIRCLE the picture that makes a rhyme. WRITE the rhyming word in the space.

The pig lost her _____.
1

My pin fell in the _____.
2

"Help me dig," said the _____.
3

Space Walk Words

Make three-letter words with short i. START on a blue planet. GO to the orange planet. Then GO to another blue planet.

WRITE the words here.

_____   _____   _____

\- \- \- \- \- \- \- \-   \- \- \- \- \- \- \- \-   \- \- \- \- \- \- \- \-

_____   _____   _____

_____   _____   _____

\- \- \- \- \- \- \- \-   \- \- \- \- \- \- \- \-   \- \- \- \- \- \- \- \-

Spell Short O

Slide Words

Let's make words that have a short **o** sound. DRAW a line between each picture and the ending that matches. Then WRITE the first letter of each word.

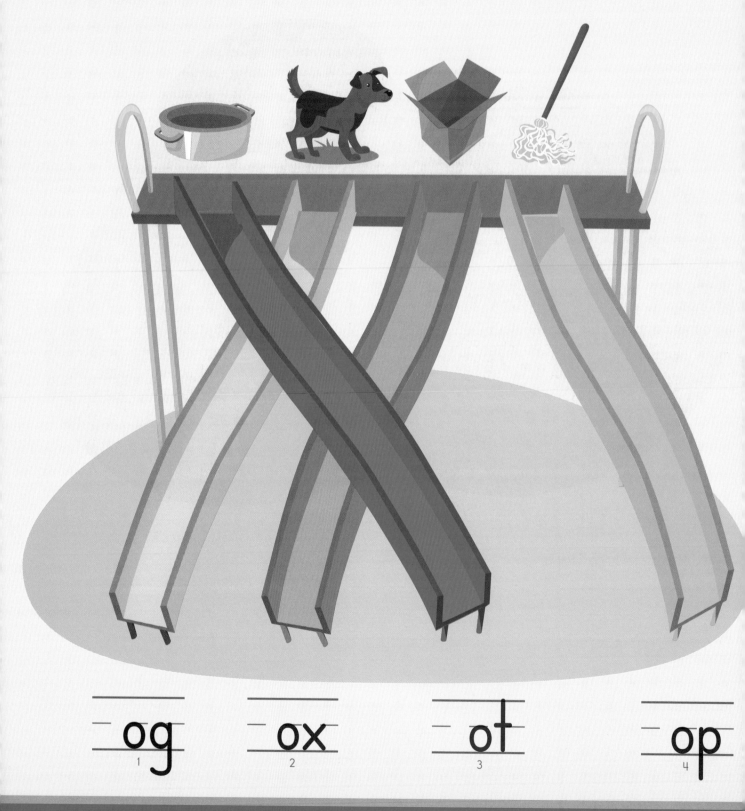

og
1

ox
2

ot
3

op
4

Letter Ladder

Let's make more words with the short **o** sound. IDENTIFY the pictures on the ladder. Then WRITE the words next to the pictures.

HINT: You can change just one letter to make each new word.

O
1

O
2

O
3

O
4

Make It Rhyme

CIRCLE the picture that makes a rhyme. WRITE the rhyming word in the space.

The dog jumps on a _____ .

The box is on top of the _____ .

Can you hop over the _____ ?

Fast Words

Can you SAY this sentence three times fast? Try it!

Hot pot tops pop.

Now WRITE your own sentence. Use these words or other short **o** words. Then SAY the sentence three times fast!

fox	box	a	mops	the

_____

_____

_____

_____

Space Walk Words

Make three-letter words with short **o**. START on a blue planet. GO to the green planet. Then GO to another blue planet.

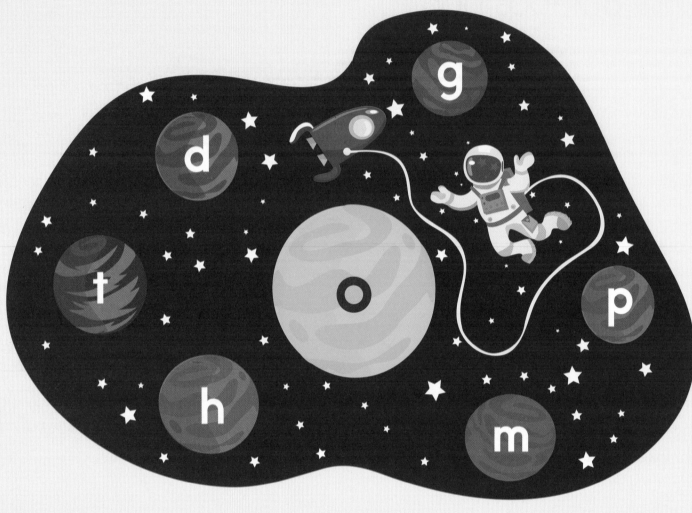

WRITE the words here.

_____   _____   _____

_ _ _ _ _ _ _ _ _   _ _ _ _ _ _ _ _ _   _ _ _ _ _ _ _ _ _

_____   _____   _____

_ _ _ _ _ _ _ _ _   _ _ _ _ _ _ _ _ _   _ _ _ _ _ _ _ _ _

Riddle Me This!

UNSCRAMBLE the words to read the riddle.

Q: What ogd pops out of a tpo

_____   _____

- - - - - - - -   - - - - - - - -

_____   _____

that is oht?

_____

- - - - - - - -

_____

A: A hot dog!

Slide Words

Let's make words that have a short **u** sound. DRAW a line between each picture and the ending that matches. Then WRITE the first letter of each word.

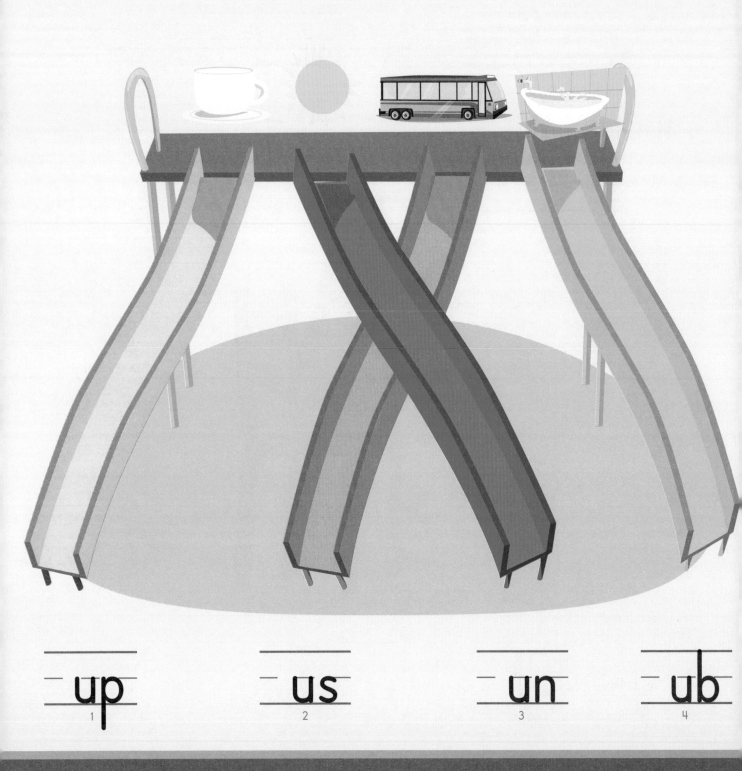

up
1

us
2

un
3

ub
4

Make It Rhyme

CIRCLE the picture that makes a rhyme. WRITE the rhyming word in the space.

The cub jumped in the _____ .
₁

The pup found a _____ .
₂

The bug hid under the _____ .
₃

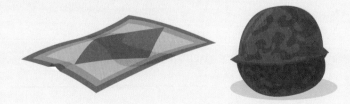

Spell Short U

Around We Go!

CIRCLE the things that have a short **u** sound.

WRITE the words with short **u** on the lines.

_____   _____   _____

_____   _____   _____

_____

Riddle Me This!

UNSCRAMBLE the words in the riddle.

Q: Why did the ubg drive

————————

————————

his usb into the btu?

———— ————

———— ————

A: To get wheel-y wet!

Space Walk Words

Make three-letter words with short **u**. START on a blue planet. GO to the green planet.
Then GO to another blue planet.

WRITE the words here.

Criss Cross

READ the clues. FILL IN the short **u** words in the boxes.

| nut | bug | tub | sun | mud | hut | bus | but | gum |

Across

1. A small house is a _____.

3. It takes kids to school.

5. A little insect

7. A _____ has a hard shell.

8. This makes pigs dirty.

Down

2. Where you take a bath

4. The _____ shines in the sky.

5. I ran fast _____ did not win the race.

6. You can chew this.

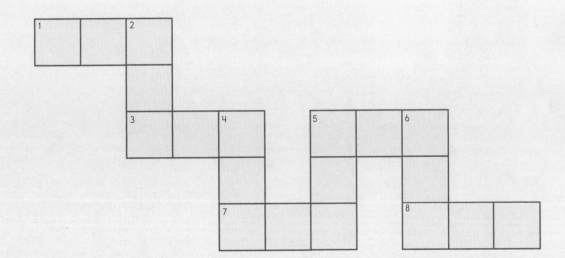

Living Colors

LOOK at all the colors in the market. WRITE a color word under each food.

| red | blue | yellow | orange | green | purple | brown | white |

1

2

3

4

5

6

7

8

Perfect Landing

DRAW a line between each word and the missing vowel. WRITE the vowel in the space.

Alphabet Soup

Use the letters in the soup to WRITE the words to match the pictures. CROSS OUT each letter in the soup after you use it.

Fix It!

CHANGE the vowels to fix the signs. WRITE the correct word under each store.

Hets

Bids

Rogs

Mups

_____

- - - - - - - -

_____

1

_____

- - - - - - - -

_____

2

_____

- - - - - - - -

_____

3

_____

- - - - - - - -

_____

4

Bubble Pop

LOOK at the color words in the bubbles. CROSS OUT the words that are misspelled.

yellow

yello

blue

gren

blu

orange

purpel

green

orang

purple

Slide Words

Let's make words that have a long **a** sound. DRAW a line between each picture and the ending that matches. Then WRITE the first letter of each word.

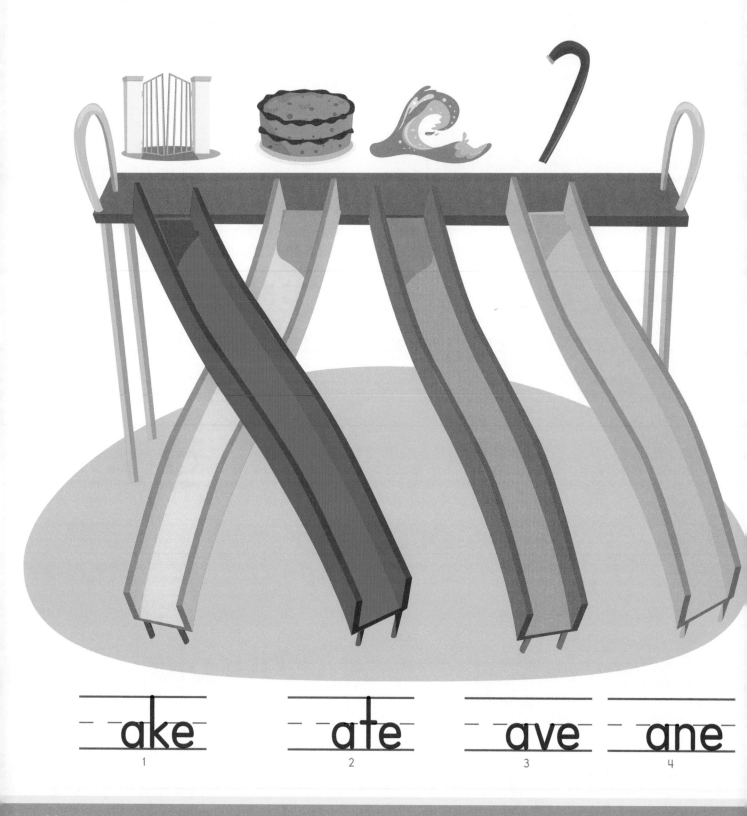

ake
1

ate
2

ave
3

ane
4

Letter Ladder

Let's make more words with the long **a** sound. IDENTIFY the pictures on the ladder. Then WRITE the words next to the pictures.

HINT: You can change just one letter to make each new word.

a e
1

a e
2

a e
3

a e
4

Spell Long A

Around We Go!

CIRCLE the things that have a long **a** sound.

WRITE the words with long **a** on the lines.

_____   _____   _____

- - - - - - - - -   - - - - - - - - -   - - - - - - - - -

_____   _____   _____

Fast Words

Can you SAY this sentence three times fast? Try it!

An ape in a cape came with a cake.

Now WRITE your own sentence. Use these words or other long **a** words. Then SAY the sentence three times fast!

| waves | save | lakes | safe |

Spell Long E and I

Slide Words

Let's make words that have a long **e** or long **i** sound. DRAW a line between each picture and the ending that matches. Then WRITE the first letter of each word.

___ine
1

___ete
2

___ite
3

___ike
4

Letter Liftoff

FILL IN the vowel for each long **e** or long **i** word.

P _ te
1

p _ pe
2

b _ ke
3

k _ te
4

n _ ne
5

Spell Long E and I

Fast Words

Can you SAY this sentence three times fast? Try it!

Five fine vines are mine.

Now WRITE your own sentence. Use these words or other long **i** words. Then SAY the sentence three times fast!

piled	tiles	Pete	wide

Criss Cross

READ the clues. FILL IN the long **e** and **i** words in the boxes.

| bike | kite | pipe | time | Pete | dime | bite | nine |

Across

2. Ten cents

3. Water goes through this to get

   to your bathtub

4. It comes before ten.

5. A clock tells you the _____.

6. A short word for *bicycle*

Down

1. This flies up in the sky.

3. A nickname for Peter

6. When you eat, you take a big _____.

Spell Long O and U

Slide Words

Let's make words that have a long **o** sound. DRAW a line between each picture and the ending that matches. Then WRITE the first letter of each word.

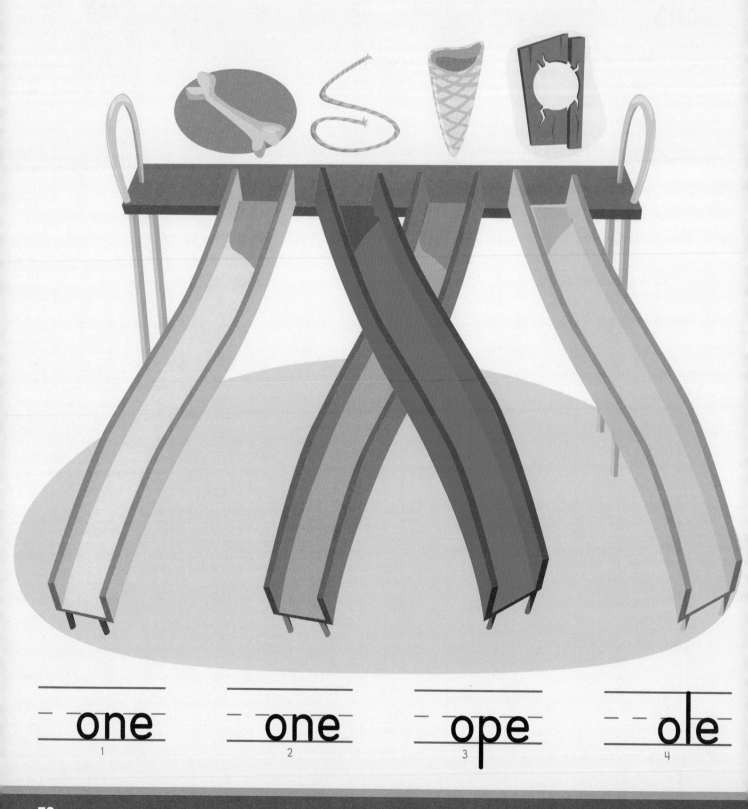

one
1

one
2

ope
3

ole
4

Fast Words

Can you SAY this sentence three times fast? Try it!

The cute duke rode and dozed.

Now WRITE your own sentence. Use these words or other long **o** or long **u** words. Then SAY the sentence three times fast!

holes   poles   homes   in   poke

Letter Liftoff

FILL IN the vowel for each long **o** or long **u** word.

h __ le
1

c __ ne
2

r __ pe
3

d __ ke
4

b __ ne
5

Riddle Me This!

UNSCRAMBLE the words in the riddle.

Q: Why did the kude put

_____

- - - - - - - -

_____

his neco on a erpo?

_____   _____

- - - - - - -   - - - - - - -

_____   _____

A: He wanted to hang onto it!

Spell Opposites

Opposites Are Everywhere!

FILL IN the word that goes with each picture.

fast or slow?

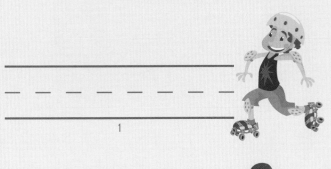

_____
- - - - - - - - - -
_____
1

_____
- - - - - - - - - -
_____
2

big or little?

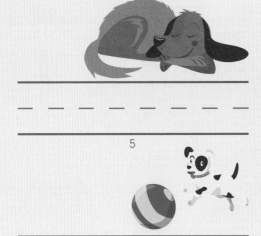

_____
- - - - - - - - - -
_____
5

_____
- - - - - - - - - -
_____
6

hot or cold?

_____
- - - - - - - - - -
_____
3

_____
- - - - - - - - - -
_____
4

short or tall?

_____
- - - - - - - - - -
_____
7

_____
- - - - - - - - - -
_____
8

Perfect Landing

DRAW a line between each word and the missing vowel. WRITE the vowel in the space.

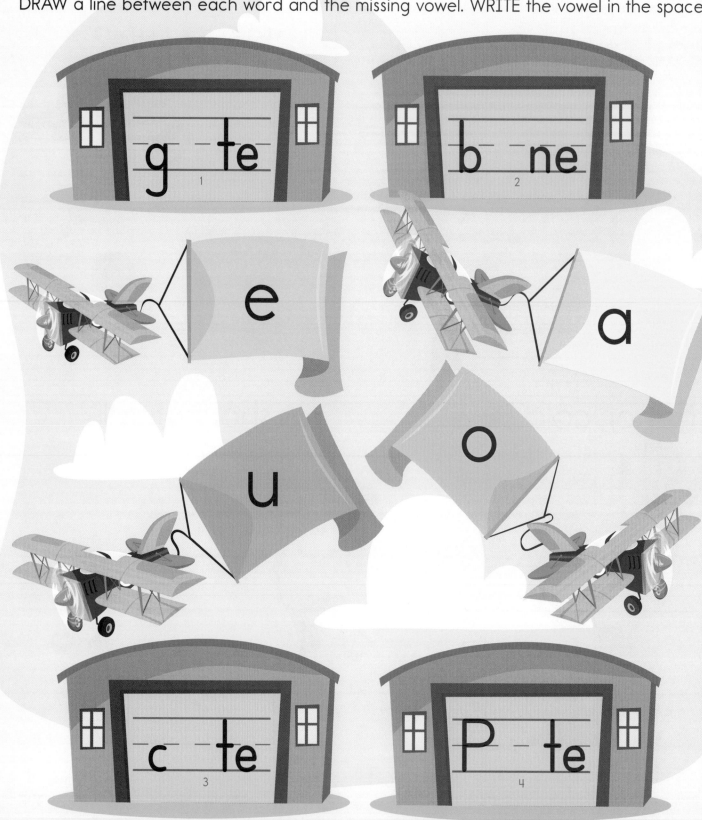

g _ te
1

b _ ne
2

e

a

u

o

c _ te
3

P _ te
4

How Does It End?

The ends of these words got chopped off. DRAW a line between the beginning and end of each word.

k	ate
v	et
f	one
w	ig
c	ox
g	ite

WRITE the words here.

_____ _____ _____

- - - - - - - - - - - - - - - - - - - - - - - - - - -

_____ _____ _____

_____ _____ _____

- - - - - - - - - - - - - - - - - - - - - - - - - - -

_____ _____ _____

Alphabet Soup

Use the letters in the soup to WRITE the words to match the pictures. CROSS OUT each letter in the soup after you use it.

Bubble Pop

LOOK at the words in the bubbles. CROSS OUT the words that are misspelled.

dook

pol

Pete

pole

lake

duke

byke

lak

Pett

bike

Fix It!

Which letters are missing from the signs? WRITE the correct word under each store.

1

2

3

4

Word Hunt

CIRCLE the **opposite** words in the grid. WRITE each word as you circle it. When you circle a word, CROSS OUT the word in the box. Words go across and down.

| big | small | slow | fast | under | over | tall | short | hot | cold |

```
s  i  l  e  u  b  f  g  c  o  l  d
h  b  t  o  n  x  s  m  a  l  l  v
o  i  a  v  d  e  l  o  f  a  s  t
r  g  l  e  e  h  o  t  w  j  o  h
t  a  l  r  r  n  w  h  x  s  v  t
```

"C" or "K"?

Slide Words

Let's make words that have the letters "c" and "k." DRAW a line between each picture and the ending that matches. Then WRITE the first letter of each word.

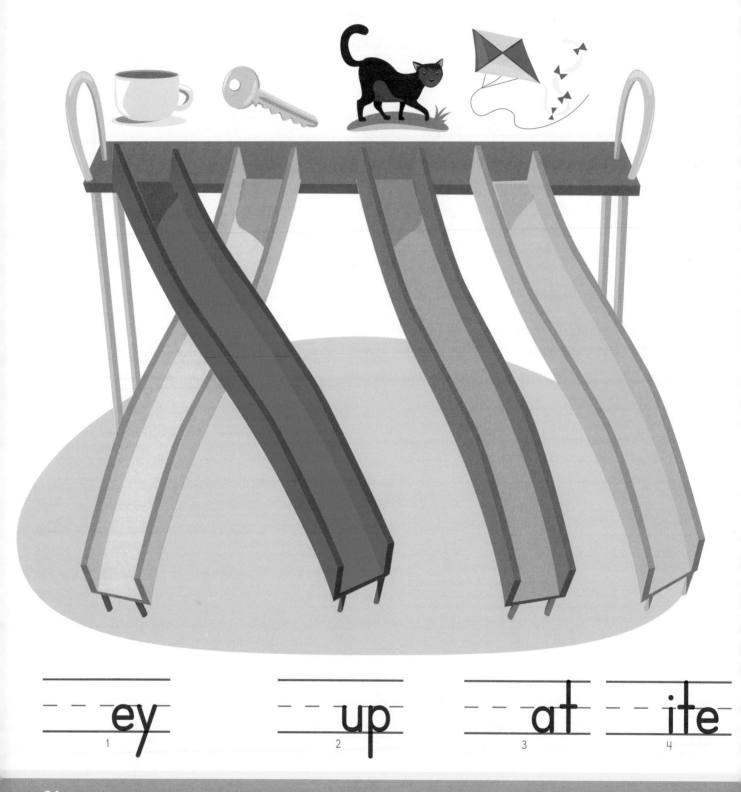

___ey
1

___up
2

___at
3

___ite
4

Letter Liftoff

FILL IN the letter "c" or "k" in each space.

bi_e
1

_ave
2

_ite
3

_one
4

_ake
5

Riddle Me This!

UNSCRAMBLE the words to read the riddle.

Q: Why did the ogd put two dils

on his edb?

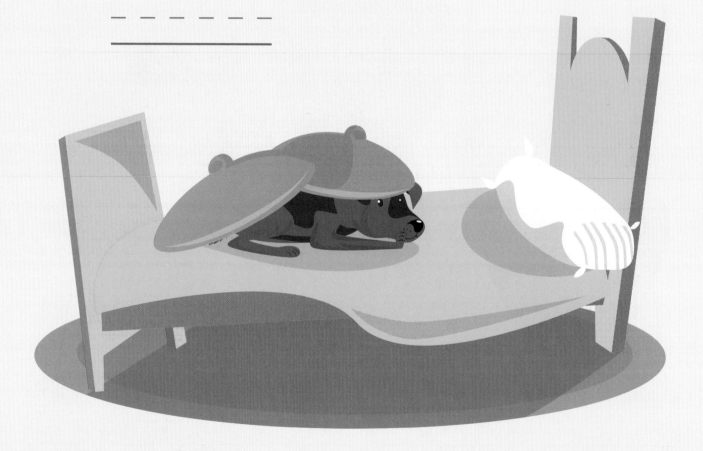

A: He wanted to sleep under the covers!

Fast Words

Can you SAY this sentence three times fast? Try it!

The bug dug big dog bones.

Now WRITE your own sentence. Use these words or other "b" or "d" words. Then SAY the sentence three times fast!

buns   bad   baked   Deb

_____

_ _

_____

_ _

_____

"B" or "P"?

Travel Tags

Let's make words that have the letters "b" and "p." Then WRITE the words in the tags.

Letter Liftoff

FILL IN the letter "b" or "p" in each space.

ta_e
1

__ike
2

pi_e
3

ro_e
4

__one
5

"S" or "Z"?

Around We Go!

CIRCLE the things that are spelled with the letter "s."

WRITE the words with "s" on the lines.

_____   _____   _____

- - - - - - - - -   - - - - - - - - -   - - - - - - - - -

_____   _____   _____

Criss Cross

READ the clues. FILL IN the words with "s" or "z" in the boxes.

doze	hose	maze	nose	rose	size

Across

4. What _____ shoe do you wear?

5. You can use a _____ to water

   the flowers.

6. When you take a nap, you _____.

Down

1. A flower that smells nice

2. You can get lost in this.

3. You use this to smell.

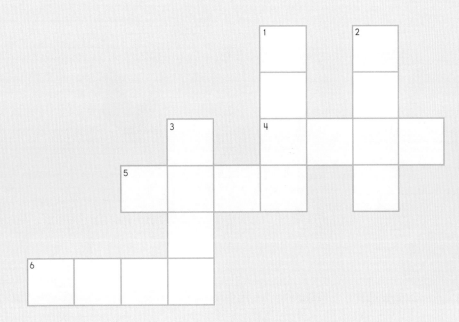

Travel Tags

Let's make words that have the letters "m" and "n." Then WRITE the words in the tags.

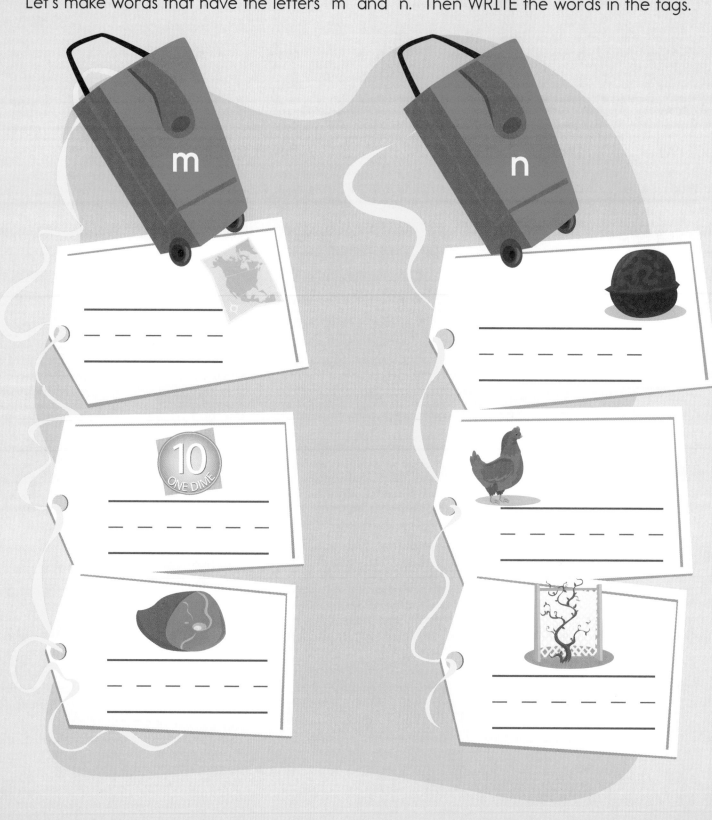

Fast Words

Can you SAY this sentence three times fast? Try it!

Nine moms ran nine miles.

Now WRITE your own sentence. Use these words or other "m" or "n" words. Then SAY the sentence three times fast!

named   mice   nine   Mike

Slide Words

Let's make words that have the letters "v" and "w." DRAW a line between each picture and the ending that matches. Then WRITE the first letter of each word.

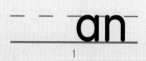 an

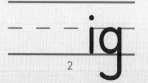 ig

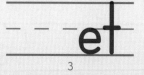 et

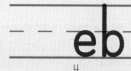 eb

1   2   3   4

Letter Liftoff

FILL IN the letter "v" or "w" in each space.

fi_e
1

_ine
2

_a_e
3

_eb
4

_ig
5

Around We Go!

CIRCLE the things that are spelled with the letter "d" or "t."

WRITE the words with "d" and "t" on the lines.

_____   _____   _____

Travel Tags

Let's make words that have the letters "d" and "t." Then WRITE the words in the tags.

Spell with Double Letters

Slide Words

Let's make words that have double letters at the end. DRAW a line between each picture and the ending that matches. Then WRITE the first letter of each word.

ell

1

oll

2

gg

3

iss

4

Fast Words

Can you SAY this sentence three times fast? Try it!

The big bell fell on Bill.

Now WRITE your own sentence. Use these words or other words with double letters. Then SAY the sentence three times fast!

| dolls | dull | less | sell |

_____

 ̄ ̄

_____

 ̄ ̄

_____

What's Happening?

FILL IN the **action** word that goes with each picture.

play or nap?

_____

- - - - - - - - - - - - -

_____

1

_____

- - - - - - - - - - - - -

_____

2

jump or stop?

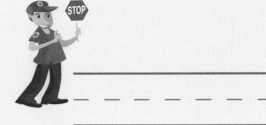

_____

- - - - - - - - - - - - -

_____

5

_____

- - - - - - - - - - - - -

_____

6

walk or skate?

_____

- - - - - - - - - - - - -

_____

3

_____

- - - - - - - - - - - - -

_____

4

eat or talk?

_____

- - - - - - - - - - - - -

_____

7

_____

- - - - - - - - - - - - -

_____

8

Perfect Landing

DRAW a line between each word and the missing letter. WRITE the letter in the space.

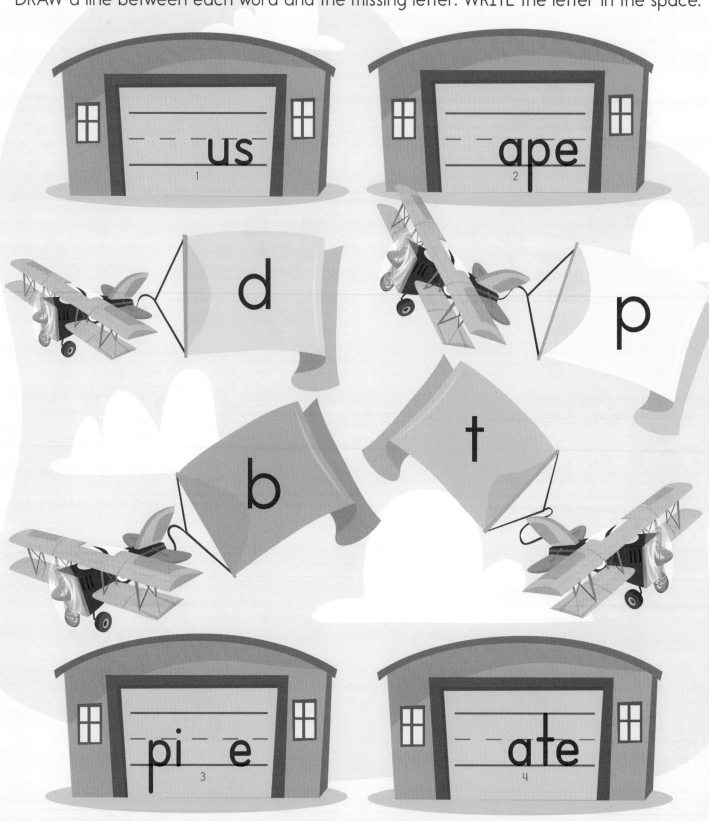

__ us
1

__ ape
2

d

p

b

t

pi __ e
3

__ ate
4

Bubble Pop

LOOK at the words in the bubbles. CROSS OUT the words that are misspelled.

maze

kite

kide

kake

map

cake

mase

mab

nose

noze

Review

Fix It!

CHANGE or ADD the letters to fix the signs. WRITE the correct word under each store.

Dols

Bess

_____

1

_____

2

Egs

Wulls

_____

3

_____

4

Bubble Pop

LOOK at the **action** words in the bubbles. CROSS OUT the words that are misspelled.

jumb

talk

eat

scate

eet

play

jump

tak

blay

skate

Spell with "-Ed" Endings

Slide Words

To make most action words happen in the past, add "-ed." DRAW a line between each picture and the ending that matches. Then WRITE the beginning of each word.

HINT: If a word has a short vowel sound, double the last letter before adding "-ed."
stop → stopped

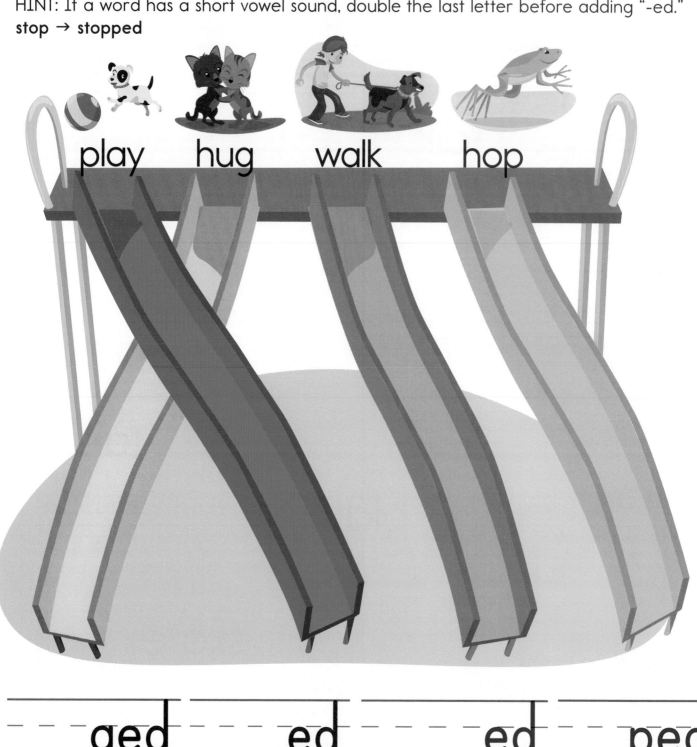

play   hug   walk   hop

ged   ed   ed   ped

1   2   3   4

Letter Liftoff

FILL IN the ending for each word to make it past tense. If a word has a short vowel sound, be sure to double the last letter before adding "-ed."

HINT: If a word has an "e" at the end, drop the "e" before adding "-ed."

wave
1

hop
2

talk
3

doze
4

hug
5

Spell with "-Ed" Endings

Travel Tags

Let's make more words past tense. DRAW a line from each suitcase to the tag that matches. Then FILL IN the missing endings.

How Does It End?

The "-ed" endings of these words got chopped off! DRAW a line between the beginning and end of each word. Then WRITE the words in the boxes.

hug	ded
bake	ped
stop	ed
talk	d
nod	ged
miss	ed

Spell with "-Ing" Endings

Letter Liftoff

Sometimes action words end with "-ing." FILL IN the "ing" ending for these words.

eat _____ 1

play _____ 2

walk _____ 3

talk _____ 4

How Does It End?

DRAW a line between the beginning and end of each word. WRITE the words in the boxes.

HINT: If a word has a short vowel sound, double the last letter before adding "-ing": hop → hopping.

run   ning

cut   ping

sit   ting

nap   bing

rub   ping

hop   ting

Tricky Endings

Try this trick for making words that end with "-ing." When a word ends with "e," take off the "e" and add "-ing": **ride → riding**

hide ➡️ _____
1

rake ➡️ _____
2

doze ➡️ _____
3

bite ➡️ _____
4

tune ➡

5

skate ➡

6

dive ➡

7

poke ➡

8

How Do You Do It?

A word that tells **how** someone does something ends with "-ly." WRITE an "-ly" word on each sign so people know what to do!

Be safe in the water.

Swim

Be nice when you talk.

Talk

Go for a slow ride.

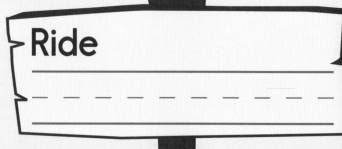

Ride

Fast Words

Can you SAY this sentence three times fast? Try it!

Nate rode slowly and safely.

Now WRITE your own sentence. Use these words or other words with "-ly." Then say the sentence fast!

nicely   kites   and   fly   wisely

Spell Animal Words

Slide Words

Let's make animal words. DRAW a line between each picture and the ending that matches. Then WRITE the first letter of each word.

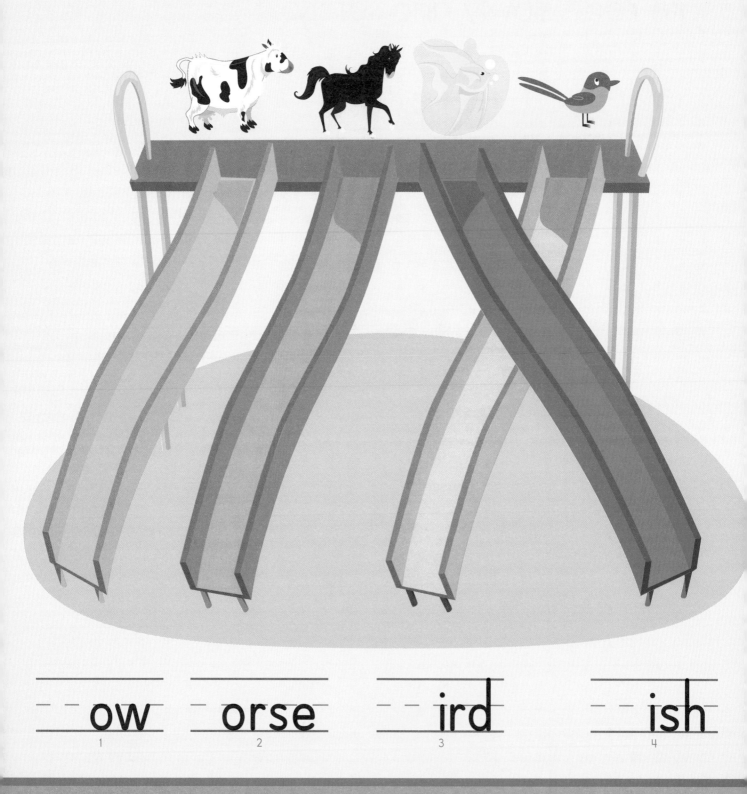

ow   orse   ird   ish

1   2   3   4

Letter Liftoff

FILL IN the beginning letter of each animal word.

___ nake
1

___ rog
2

___ ion
3

___ ouse
4

___ oat
5

Review

Soccer Star

DRAW a line between each picture and the end of the word to make it past tense. WRITE the words in the nets.

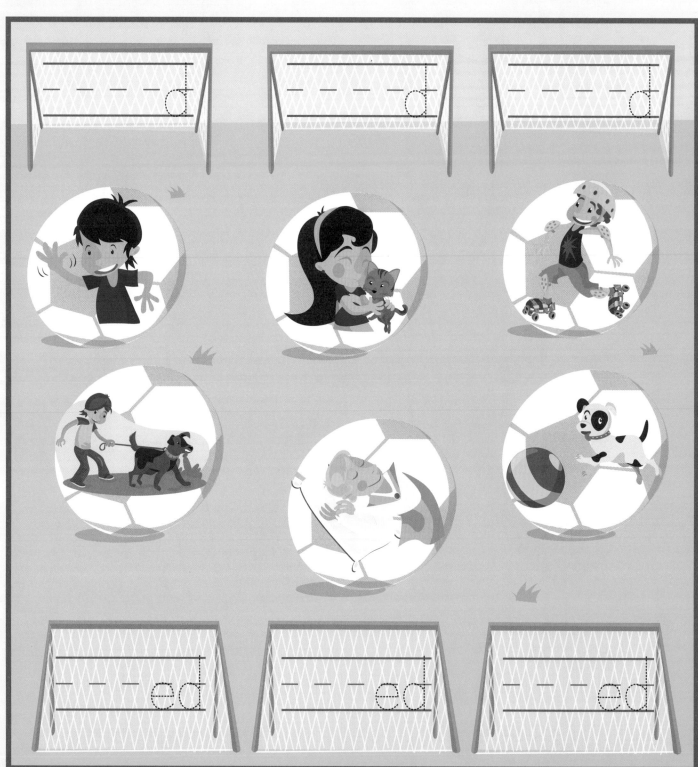

98

Fix It!

One word on each sign is misspelled. WRITE the correct word under each store.

1

2

3

4

Bubble Pop

LOOK at the words in the bubbles. CROSS OUT the words that are misspelled.

badly

nicley

safly

nicely

slowly

wiseley

badley

wisely

safely

slowely

Word Hunt

CIRCLE the **animal words** in the grid. WRITE each word as you circle it. When you circle a word, CROSS OUT the word in the box. Words go across and down.

| cow | horse | frog | bird | goat | mouse | snake | fish | lion | cat |

```
l  i  o  n  n  m  s  h  a  l  s  v
p  u  f  m  b  o  g  o  a  t  n  f
g  t  r  l  i  u  o  r  c  j  a  i
x  c  o  w  r  s  p  s  a  d  k  s
o  l  g  s  d  e  r  e  t  i  e  h
```

Spell Plurals

Letter Liftoff

Plural means "more than one." When a word tells about more than one thing, add an "-s": **hat → hats**

WRITE plural words. ADD an "-s" to each word.

bird
1

kite
2

egg
3

bone
4

cat
5

Tricky Endings

If a word ends with "x" or "s," to make it plural, add "-es": **box→boxes**

Try it! WRITE plural words by adding "-es" to these words.

bus ➜

_____
- - - - - - - - - - -
_____
1

fox ➜

_____
- - - - - - - - - - -
_____
2

kiss ➜

_____
- - - - - - - - - - -
_____
3

mess ➜

_____
- - - - - - - - - - -
_____
4

box ➜

_____
- - - - - - - - - - -
_____
5

What Do You See at the Party?

What do you see at Kate's birthday party? FILL IN the blanks using **plural** words.

| cakes | kisses | hats | boxes | cups | buses |

1. There are two pink birthday _____ on the table.

2. The kids are wearing _____ with dots on them.

3. The _____ have presents inside.

4. The blue _____ are on the table too.

5. Tim is playing with yellow toy _____ .

6. Kate's mother and father are giving her

_____ .

Getting to Know You

Some words that end with "-er" tell about people. WRITE the word that matches each person.

eater	jumper	kisser	talker	walker

1

2

3

4

5

What Do You Do?

WRITE "-er" words that tell about these people.

HINT: When a word ends with an "e," drop the "e" before adding "-er."

1. If you **bake** a cake, you are a _____.

2. If you work in a **mine**, you are a _____.

3. If you ride your **bike**, you are a _____.

4. If you like to **skate**, you are a _____.

5. If you **rope** cows, you are a _____.

6. If you **dive** into the water, you are a _____.

People Words with "-Er"

How Does It End?

DRAW a line between each word and its "-er" ending. WRITE the words in the boxes.

HINT: When a word has a short vowel sound, double the last letter before adding "-er."

swim   ger

hop   per

win   ner

sit   mer

hug   ter

nap   per

Criss Cross

READ the clues. FILL IN the people words in the boxes.

| teacher | baker | eater | talker | diver | digger | skater |

Across

2. A person who bakes cakes

3. He likes to skate.

4. A person who digs

6. Someone who teaches

Down

1. A person who talks and talks

4. She dives into the pool.

5. Someone who eats

Look and Compare

Add "-er" at the end of describing words to compare two things. WRITE the "-er" word that tells about each person or animal.

bigger or smaller?

_____

- - - - - - - - - - - - - - - -

_____
1

_____

- - - - - - - - - - - - - - - -

_____
2

shorter or taller?

_____

- - - - - - - - - - - - - - - -

_____
5

_____

- - - - - - - - - - - - - - - -

_____
6

faster or slower?

_____

- - - - - - - - - - - - - - - -

_____
3

_____

- - - - - - - - - - - - - - - -

_____
4

hotter or colder?

_____

- - - - - - - - - - - - - - - -

_____
7

_____

- - - - - - - - - - - - - - - -

_____
8

27

Compare the Racers

Add "-est" at the end of a describing word when you compare more than two things. FILL IN the "-est" word that tells about each car in the race.

slowest   fastest   biggest   smallest   hottest   wettest

Finish

_____ 1

_____ 2

_____ 3

_____ 4

_____ 5

_____ 6

Letter Liftoff

Who are these people? FILL IN the first letter of each word.

_aby
1

_irl
2

_oy
3

_an
4

_ady
5

Criss Cross

READ the clues. FILL IN the people words in the boxes.

mother	boys	sister	man	baby	girl	father

Across

2. The opposite of *girls* is _____.

5. Another word for *dad* is _____.

6. Another word for *mom* is _____.

Down

1. A _____ is very little.

3. The opposite of *brother* is _____.

4. A _____ will grow up to be a lady.

6. Your father is a _____.

Fix It!

CHANGE or ADD vowels to fix the signs. WRITE the correct words under each store.

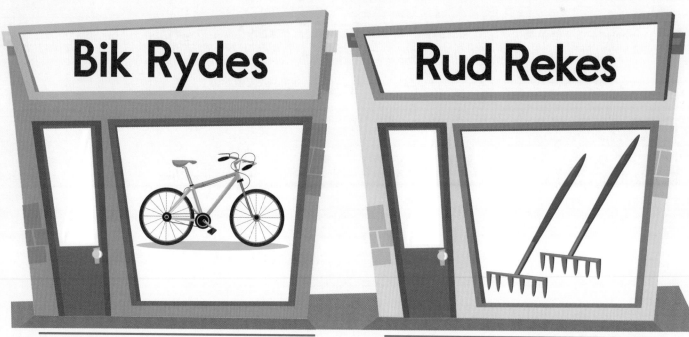

Bik Rydes

Rud Rekes

_____

_____

1

_____

_____

2

Fesh Nots

Dag Bids

_____

_____

3

_____

_____

4

Perfect Landing

DRAW a line between each word and the missing letter. Use each letter only once.
WRITE the missing letter in the space.

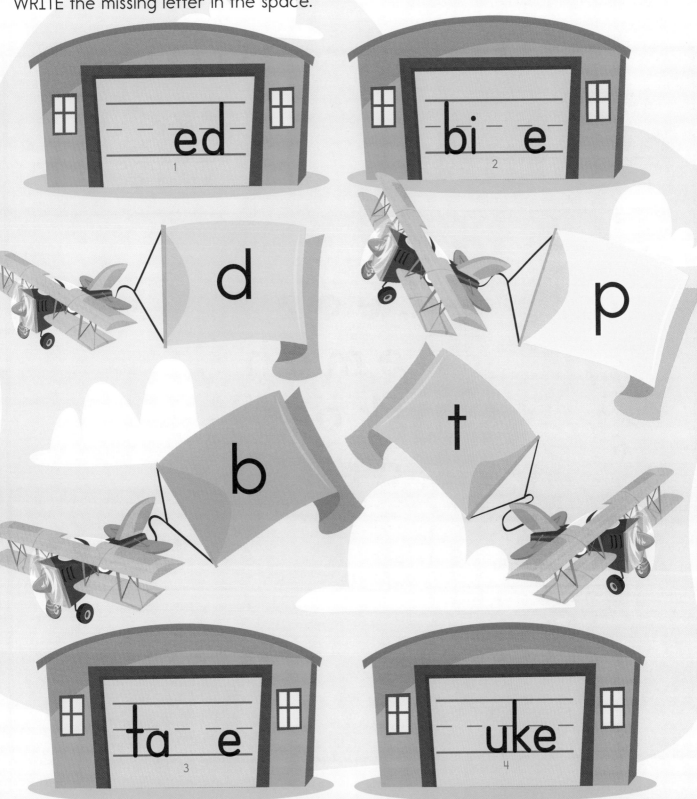

Alphabet Soup

Use the letters in the soup to WRITE the words to match the pictures. CROSS OUT each letter in the soup after you use it.

Bubble Pop

LOOK at the words in the bubbles. CROSS OUT the words that are misspelled.

stoped

talkng

rakd

raked

hiding

hideing

slowley

slowly

talking

stopped

Soccer Star

Make a noun plural by adding "-s" or "-es." DRAW a line between each picture and the end of the word. WRITE the plural words in the nets.

Word Hunt

CIRCLE the **people** words in the grid. WRITE each word as you circle it. When you circle a word, CROSS OUT the word in the box. Words go across and down.

mother	boy	baby	skater	teacher
father	girl	swimmer	baker	talker

```
t e a c h e r b a b y g
b i f a t h e r k a h i
s k a t e r t a l k e r
m b o y t m o t h e r l
h g c s w i m m e r t h
```

Answers

Page 2
1. ram
2. cat
3. map
4. fan

Page 3
Suggestion: The man and the ram ran.

Page 4
1. ram
2. rat
3. hat
4. bat

Page 5

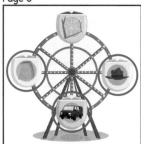

hat, van, bag

Page 6
1. The ram eats a **yam**.
2. The fan cools the **man**.
3. The hat is on the **cat**.

Page 7
Suggestions: bag, bat, cat, gab, gas, rag, rat, sag, sat, tab, tag

Page 8
1. pen
2. leg
3. bed
4. vet

Page 9
1. hen
2. bed
3. ten
4. pen
5. net

Page 10

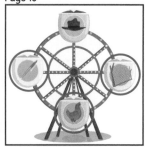

web, hen, pen

Page 11
Suggestion: Red beds have red legs.

Page 12
1. The wet pet saw the **vet**.
2. The hen has a **pen**.
3. The bed was **red**.

Page 13
Suggestions: bed, bet, den, jet, men, met, net, ten, Jeb, Jed, Deb, Ted, Ned

Pages 14-15
1. one
2. two
3. three
4. four
5. five
6. six
7. seven
8. eight

Page 16
1. net
2. hat
3. jet
4. van

Page 17
a: bat, cat, fan
e: bed, hen, vet

Page 18
1. one
2. four
3. six
4. ten

Page 19

Page 20
1. six
2. wig
3. bib
4. pin

Page 21

wig, bin, pig

Page 22
Suggestion: Pigs dig big kids.

Page 23
1. dig
2. pig
3. pin
4. bin

Page 24
1. The pig lost her **wig**.
2. My pin fell in the **bin**.
3. "Help me dig," said the **pig**.

Page 25
Suggestions: big, bin, bit, nib, nip, nit, pig, pin, pit, tip, tin, wig, win, wit

Page 26
1. dog
2. box
3. pot
4. mop

Page 27
1. pot
2. dot
3. dog
4. log

Page 28
1. The dog jumps on a **log**.
2. The box is on top of the **fox**.
3. Can you hop over the **top**?

Page 29
Suggestion: The fox mops a box.

Page 30
Suggestions: dog, dot, god, got, hog, hop, hot, mop, pod, pot, top, Tom

Page 31
Q. What **dog** pops out of a **pot** that is **hot**?

Page 32
1. cup
2. bus
3. sun
4. tub

Page 33
1. The cub jumped in the **tub**.
2. The pup found a **cup**.
3. The bug hid under the **rug**.

Page 34

cup, duck, sun

Page 35
Q: Why did the **bug** drive his **bus** into the **tub**?
Note: *bus* or *sub* works, but *bus* matches the picture.

Page 36
Suggestions: bug, bum, bun, bus, gum, gun, Gus, mug, rub, rug, run, sub, sum, sun

Page 37

ACROSS	DOWN
1. hut	2. tub
3. bus	4. sun
5. bug	5. but
7. nut	6. gum
8. mud	

Pages 38-39
1. green
2. blue
3. brown
4. red
5. yellow
6. white
7. purple
8. orange

Page 40
1. pin
2. box
3. mud
4. mom

Page 41
1. pig
2. fox
3. tub
4. bus

Page 42
1. Hets →Hats
2. Bids →Beds
3. Rogs →Rugs
4. Mups →Mops

Page 43
Misspelled Words: blu, purpel, yello, gren, orang

Page 44
1. cake
2. gate
3. wave
4. cane

Page 45
1. wave
2. cave
3. cane
4. cape

Page 46

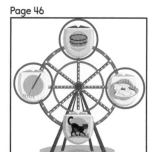

rake, cake, lake

Page 47
Suggestion: Safe waves save lakes.

Page 48
1. vine
2. Pete
3. kite
4. bike

Page 49
1. Pete
2. pipe
3. bike
4. kite
5. nine

Page 50
Suggestion: Pete piled wide tiles.

Page 51

ACROSS	DOWN
2. dime	1. kite
3. pipe	3. Pete
4. nine	6. bite
5. time	
6. bike	

Page 52
1. bone
2. cone
3. rope
4. hole

Page 53
Suggestion: Poles poke holes in homes.

Page 54
1. hole
2. cone
3. rope
4. duke
5. bone

Page 55
Q: Why did the **duke** put his **cone** on a **rope**?

Pages 56-57
1. fast
2. slow
3. cold
4. hot
5. big
6. little
7. tall
8. short

Page 58
1. gate
2. bone
3. cute
4. Pete

Page 59
kite, vet, fox, wig, cone, gate
Note: You can make *fate, fig, fox, wet, wig, gate, get, gone, gig* too, but you'll have leftover beginnings or ends.

Page 60
1. duke
2. gate
3. pipe
4. rope

Page 61
Misspelled Words: dook, pol, byke, Pett, lak

Page 62
1. __tes →Gates
2. __kes →Bikes
3. __nes →Cones
4. __kes →Rakes

Page 63

Page 64
1. key
2. cup
3. cat
4. kite

Page 65
1. bike
2. cave
3. kite
4. cone
5. cake

Page 66
Q: Why did the **dog** put two **lids** on his **bed**?

Page 67
Suggestion: Deb baked bad buns.

Page 68
b: tub, bib, web
p: map, cup, pot

Page 69
1. tape
2. bike
3. pipe
4. rope
5. bone

Page 70

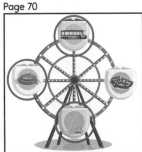

hose, bus, nose

Page 71

ACROSS	DOWN
4. size	1. rose
5. hose	2. maze
6. doze	3. nose

Page 72
m: map, dime, ham
n: nut, hen, vine

Page 73
Suggestion: Mike named nine mice.

Page 74
1. van
2. wig
3. vet
4. web

Page 75
1. five
2. vine
3. wave
4. web
5. wig

Page 76

bed, cat, top

Page 77
d: dive, dime, bed
t: tape, kite, net

Page 78
1. bell
2. doll
3. egg
4. kiss

Page 79
Suggestion: Dull dolls sell less.

Pages 80-81
1. nap
2. play
3. walk
4. skate
5. stop
6. jump
7. eat
8. talk

Page 82
1. **b**us
2. **t**ape
3. pipe
4. **d**ate

Page 83
Misspelled Words: mase, noze, kake, mab, kide

Page 84
1. Dols →Dolls
2. Bess →Bells
3. Egs →Eggs
4. Wulls →Wells

Page 85
Misspelled Words: scate , tak, eet, jumb, blay

Page 86
1. hugged
2. played
3. walked
4. hopped

Page 87
1. waved
2. hopped
3. talked
4. dozed
5. hugged

Page 88
-ed: played, walked
Drop the "e": waved skated

Page 89
hugged, baked, stopped, talked, nodded, missed

Page 90
1. eating
2. playing
3. walking
4. talking

Page 91
running, cutting, sitting, napping, rubbing, hopping

Pages 92-93
1. hide →hiding
2. rake →raking
3. doze →dozing
4. bite →biting
5. tune →tuning
6. skate →skating
7. dive →diving
8. poke →poking

Page 94
1. Swim **Safely**
2. Talk **Nicely**
3. Ride **Slowly**

Page 95
Suggestion: Fly kites nicely and wisely.

Page 96
1. cow
2. horse
3. bird
4. fish

Page 97
1. snake
2. frog
3. lion
4. mouse
5. goat

Page 98
-d: waved, skated, dozed
-ed: walked, kissed, played

Page 99
1. Cuting →Cutting
2. Bakeng →Baking
3. Rideing →Riding
4. Fixng →Fixing

Page 100
Misspelled Words: slowely, safly, wiseley, badley, nicley

Page 101

Answers

Page 102
1. birds
2. kites
3. eggs
4. bones
5. cats

Page 103
1. buses
2. foxes
3. kisses
4. messes
5. boxes

Pages 104-105
1. cakes
2. hats
3. boxes
4. cups
5. buses
6. kisses

Page 106
1. eater
2. jumper
3. walker
4. kisser
5. talker

Page 107
1. baker
2. miner
3. biker
4. skater
5. roper
6. diver

Page 108
swimmer, hopper, winner, sitter, hugger, napper

Page 109
ACROSS
2. baker
3. skater
4. digger
6. teacher

DOWN
1. talker
4. diver
5. eater

Page 110
1. bigger
2. smaller
3. slower
4. faster
5. shorter
6. taller
7. colder
8. hotter

Page 111
1. biggest
2. slowest
3. smallest
4. hottest
5. wettest
6. fastest

Page 112
1. baby
2. girl
3. boy
4. man
5. lady

Page 113
ACROSS
2. boys
5. father
6. mother

DOWN
1. baby
3. sister
4. girl
6. man

Page 114
1. Bik Rydes → Bike Rides
2. Rud Rekes → Red Rakes
3. Fesh Nots → Fish Nets
4. Dag Bids → Dog Beds

Page 115
1. bed
2. bite
3. tape
4. duke

Page 116
1. cone
2. rake
3. hose
4. maze

Page 117
Misspelled words: hideing, stoped, slowley, rakd, talkng

Page 118
-s: birds, eggs, cows
-es: buses, foxes, boxes

Page 119

122